Connect
Workbook

W0079601

Jack C. Richards
Carlos Barbisan
2
with **Chuck Sandy**
and **Dorothy E. Zemach**

CAMBRIDGE
UNIVERSITY PRESS

PUBLISHED BY THE PRESS SYNDICATE OF THE UNIVERSITY OF CAMBRIDGE
The Pitt Building, Trumpington Street, Cambridge, United Kingdom

CAMBRIDGE UNIVERSITY PRESS
The Edinburgh Building, Cambridge CB2 2RU, UK
40 West 20th Street, New York, NY 10011–4211, USA
477 Williamstown Road, Port Melbourne, VIC 3207, Australia
Ruiz de Alarcón 13, 28014 Madrid, Spain
Dock House, The Waterfront, Cape Town 8001, South Africa

http://www.cambridge.org

First published 2004
Printed in China
Typeface New Century Schoolbook   *System* QuarkXPress®

ISBN 0 521 59498 7 Student's Book 1 (English)
ISBN 0 521 60074 X Student's Book 1 (Portuguese)
ISBN 0 521 59495 2 Workbook 1 (English)
ISBN 0 521 60070 7 Workbook 1 (Portuguese)
ISBN 0 521 59494 4 Teacher's Edition 1 (English)
ISBN 0 521 59492 8 Teacher's Edition 1 (Portuguese)
ISBN 0 521 59491 X Class Audio Cassettes 1
ISBN 0 521 59488 X Class CD 1
ISBN 0 521 59487 1 Student's Book 2 (English)
ISBN 0 521 60073 1 Student's Book 2 (Portuguese)
ISBN 0 521 59484 7 Workbook 2 (English)
ISBN 0 521 60069 3 Workbook 2 (Portuguese)
ISBN 0 521 59493 6 Teacher's Edition 2 (English)
ISBN 0 521 59481 2 Teacher's Edition 2 (Portuguese)
ISBN 0 521 59480 4 Class Audio Cassettes 2
ISBN 0 521 59477 4 Class CD 2

ISBN 0 521 59476 6 Student's Book 3 (English)
ISBN 0 521 60072 3 Student's Book 3 (Portuguese)
ISBN 0 521 59475 8 Workbook 3 (English)
ISBN 0 521 60068 5 Workbook 3 (Portuguese)
ISBN 0 521 59483 9 Teacher's Edition 3 (English)
ISBN 0 521 59474 X Teacher's Edition 3 (Portuguese)
ISBN 0 521 59473 1 Class Audio Cassettes 3
ISBN 0 521 59471 5 Class CD 3
ISBN 0 521 59470 7 Student's Book 4 (English)
ISBN 0 521 60071 5 Student's Book 4 (Portuguese)
ISBN 0 521 59469 3 Workbook 4 (English)
ISBN 0 521 60064 2 Workbook 4 (Portuguese)
ISBN 0 521 59482 0 Teacher's Edition 4 (English)
ISBN 0 521 59468 5 Teacher's Edition 4 (Portuguese)
ISBN 0 521 59467 7 Class Audio Cassettes 4
ISBN 0 521 59464 2 Class CD 4

Art direction, book design, and layout services: Adventure House, NYC

Table of Contents

New friends

1 Complete the questions. Then answer the questions.

1. _Where_ are you from?
   I'm from Brazil.

2. _____ old is your best friend?
   _____

3. _____ your birthday?
   _____

4. _____ Rio de Janeiro in Mexico?
   _____

5. _____ you on the soccer team?
   _____

6. _____ Tokyo?
   _____

7. _____ your name?
   _____

8. _____ your best friend from?
   _____

2 Write questions and answers.

1. **Q:** where / San Francisco _Where's San Francisco?_
   A: California _It's in California._

2. **Q:** who / they _____
   A: my / classmates _____

3. **Q:** how / old / Angelo _____
   A: thirteen _____

4. **Q:** you / in / Sabrina's class _____
   A: yes _____

5. **Q:** your / name _____
   A: Nina / not Samantha _____
   _____

6. **Q:** who / she _____
   A: my science teacher / not my English teacher
   _____

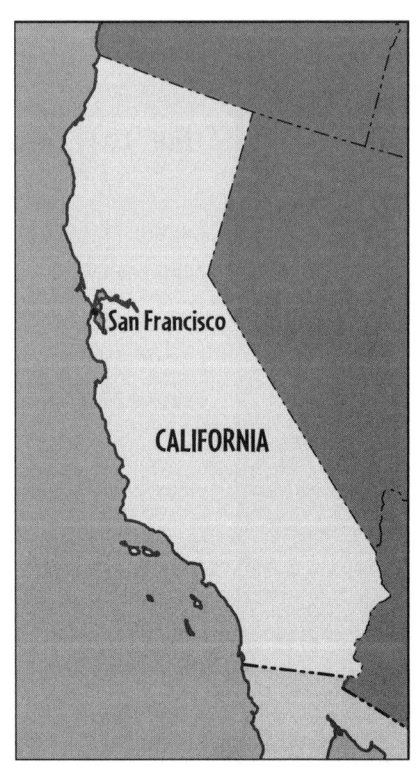

Lesson 2 Neighborhoods

1 Complete the conversation with the words in the box.

☐ Are there any   ☐ there are   ☐ There aren't   ☐ there isn't
☑ Is there a   ☐ There are no   ☐ there is a   ☐ There's no

Beth   Hi, Tasha. What's your new school like?

Tasha   Well, it's not very big, but it's nice.

Beth   *Is there a* swimming pool?

Tasha   No, _____ . But _____
swimming pool in my neighborhood.

Beth   _____ tennis courts?

Tasha   Yes, _____ . _____ basketball
courts, though. That's OK, because I can't
play basketball!

Beth   Where's the mall? Is it near your school?

Tasha   _____ mall near my school. _____
any stores near my school, either.

Beth   Too bad!

2 Write questions. Then answer the questions with information about your neighborhood.

1. **Q:** (parks) *Are there any parks?*
   A: *Yes, there are.*

2. **Q:** (big library) _____
   A: _____

3. **Q:** (movie theater) _____
   A: _____

4. **Q:** (tennis courts) _____
   A: _____

5. **Q:** (shoe stores) _____
   A: _____

6. **Q:** (gym) _____
   A: _____

7. **Q:** (restaurants) _____
   A: _____

8. **Q:** (skating rink) _____
   A: _____

1 Unscramble the questions. Then match the questions to the answers.

1. they / who / are ?
   Who are they? ____ _b_

2. a / in / neighborhood / library / Is / your / there ?
   _____ ____

3. your / What's / name ?
   _____ ____

4. any / baseball fields / at / Are / your / there / school ?
   _____ ____

5. from / she / Puerto Rico / Is ?
   _____ ____

6. are / you / from / Where ?
   _____ ____

a. There are no baseball fields at my school.

b. They're my brothers.

c. No, she's not.

d. Yes, there is.

e. I'm from Venezuela.

f. My name's Hector.

2 Answer the questions.

1. **Q:** Is there a skating rink in the park?
   A: (yes) _Yes, there is._

2. **Q:** How old is Bayardo?
   A: (twelve / not thirteen) _____

3. **Q:** When's your birthday?
   A: (December / not May) _____

4. **Q:** Is there a gym in your school?
   A: (no) _____

5. **Q:** Are you in Mrs. Giavatto's history class?
   A: (no / Mr. Valli) _____

6. **Q:** Who are they?
   A: (not my teachers / my parents) _____

1 Number the sentences in the correct order.

_____ Wow! He's good at tennis.

_____ And who's that?

_____ Yes, he's really athletic. He's also pretty good at soccer and baseball.

_____ That's Rico's friend, Steve.

_____ Hi, Brian. Who's that?

_____ He's not good at tennis.

_____ Hello, Jenna. That's my friend, Rico.

_____ You're right. But he can tell great jokes. He's funny.

2 Complete the sentences with the words in the box.

☐ artistic ☐ draw ☐ funny ☑ musical
☐ athletic ☐ friendly ☐ languages ☐ smart

1. She can play a lot of instruments.
   She's _musical_ .

2. He can make friends easily.
   He's _____.

3. She's good at drawing.
   She's _____.

4. She can tell great jokes.
   She's really _____.

5. He's good at soccer and volleyball.
   He's _____.

6. She's good at math, computers, and English.
   She's _____.

7. He can speak four _____.

8. I can _____ great pictures.

3 Write sentences with *good at*, *pretty good at*, and *not good at* about people you know.

1. (English) _Lisa's not good at English._   4. (science) _____

2. (painting) _____   5. (math) _____

3. (music) _____   6. (sports) _____

4 Our pets

1 Choose the correct words to complete the conversations.

1. **A** Spiders are cool. I like spiders _____*a lot*_____ (a little / a lot).

   B Not me. I don't like spiders _____ (a lot / at all).

2. **A** I don't like parrots _____ (a little / very much).

   B Really? Parrots are active. I like parrots _____ (a lot / at all).

3. **A** Spiders are dangerous. I don't like spiders _____ (a little / at all).

   B Spiders are OK. I like spiders _____ (a little / a lot).

4. **A** Cats are boring and messy. I don't like cats _____ (a lot / very much).

   B Oh, cats aren't bad. I like cats _____ (very much / a little).

2 Match the pictures to the correct conversations in part 1. Write the correct numbers in the boxes.

4

3 What do you think of these animals and things? Do you like them? Answer with your own information.

1. (cats) *Cats are cute. I like cats a lot.*

2. (music stores) _____

3. (concerts) _____

4. (dogs) _____

5. (video games) _____

6. (comic books) _____

7. (computers) _____

8. (parrots) _____

Lesson 5 Connections

1 Complete the information on the class Web page. Use more than one word when necessary.

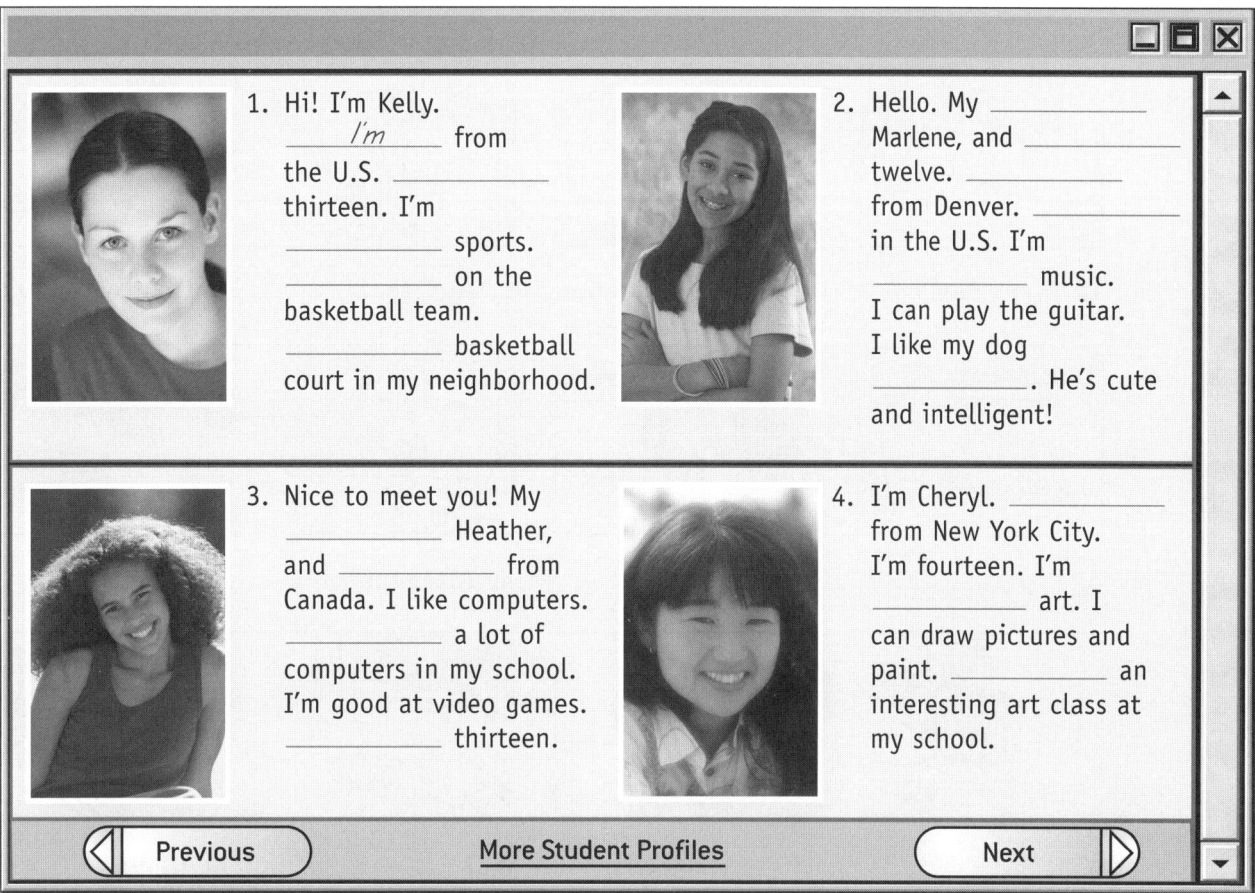

1. Hi! I'm Kelly. _____*I'm*_____ from the U.S. _____ thirteen. I'm _____ sports. _____ on the basketball team. _____ basketball court in my neighborhood.

2. Hello. My _____ Marlene, and _____ twelve. _____ from Denver. _____ in the U.S. I'm _____ music. I can play the guitar. I like my dog _____. He's cute and intelligent!

3. Nice to meet you! My _____ Heather, and _____ from Canada. I like computers. _____ a lot of computers in my school. I'm good at video games. _____ thirteen.

4. I'm Cheryl. _____ from New York City. I'm fourteen. I'm _____ art. I can draw pictures and paint. _____ an interesting art class at my school.

◁ Previous   **More Student Profiles**   Next ▷

2 Look at part 1. Who are these sentences about? Check (✓) the correct names.

	Kelly	Marlene	Heather	Cheryl
1. She's twelve.	☐	☑	☐	☐
2. She's athletic.	☐	☐	☐	☐
3. She's good at computers.	☐	☐	☐	☐
4. She's not from the U.S.	☐	☐	☐	☐
5. She's artistic.	☐	☐	☐	☐

3 Write questions.

1. **Q:** _*Where's New York City?*_ **A:** New York City? It's in the United States.

2. **Q:** _____ **A:** My birthday's in April.

3. **Q:** _____ **A:** Yes, there are. There are four tennis courts in my neighborhood.

4. **Q:** _____ **A:** He's my science teacher.

5. **Q:** _____ **A:** They're my classmates.

1 Complete the sentences about Eduardo's day with the words in the box.

☐ do homework ☐ eat breakfast ☐ eat dinner ☑ get up ☐ go to bed ☐ go to school

1. Every day, I ____*get up*____ at 7:00.

2. At 7:45, I _____ with my family.

3. I _____ with my friends.

4. After school, I _____ .

5. I _____ with my sister.

6. I _____ at 10:00.

2 Write sentences.   👍 = things I do   👎 = things I don't do

1. get up / 7:00 👍 / 8:00 👎

   I get up at 7:00. I don't get up at 8:00.

2. eat breakfast / with my friends 👎 / with my family 👍

   _____

3. eat lunch / cafeteria 👍 / home 👎

   _____

4. do my homework / school 👎 / home 👍

   _____

5. watch TV / with my friends 👍 / with my teachers 👎

   _____

6. go to bed / 10:30 👍 / 11:30 👎

   _____

Free time

1 Complete the conversations with the words in the box and *Do you*; *Yes, I do*; or *No, I don't*.

☑ collect   ☐ listen   ☐ take   ☐ watch
☐ hang out   ☐ play   ☐ talk   ☐ write

1. **A** _Do you collect_____ trading cards?

   B _Yes, I do.____ I collect baseball trading cards.

2. **A** _____ sports?

   B _____ I'm not very athletic.

3. **A** _____ at the mall after school?

   B _____ I go home after school.

4. **A** _____ to music?

   B _____ My favorite singer is Shakira.

5. **A** _____ music lessons?

   B _____ I take piano lessons.

6. **A** _____ DVDs?

   B _____ DVDs are boring.

7. **A** _____ e-mail messages?

   B _____ I write e-mail messages every day!

8. **A** _____ on the phone?

   B _____ I talk on the phone with my friends every day!

2 Unscramble the questions. Then match the questions to the answers.

1. take / you / guitar / Do / lessons ?
   _Do you take guitar lessons?____ _f_

   a. Yes, I do. I'm pretty good at soccer.

2. Internet / you / the / Do / use ?
   _____ ___

   b. No, I don't. I hang out at home.

3. soccer / Do / play / you ?
   _____ ___

   c. No, I don't. I can't dance at all.

4. at / hang out / the / Do / you / mall ?
   _____ ___

   d. Yes, I do. My favorite singer is Madonna.

5. to / you / music / Do / listen ?
   _____ ___

   e. No, I don't. I don't have a computer.

6. lessons / Do / dance / take / you ?
   _____ ___

   f. No, I don't. I take piano lessons.

Mini-review

1 Check (✓) the word or phrase that is different. Then write one more correct word or phrase.

1. ☐ in-line skate ☐ dance ☑ use the Internet ☐ play soccer *play tennis*
2. ☐ listen ☐ videos ☐ watch ☐ talk _____
3. ☐ collect stamps ☐ get up ☐ go to school ☐ go home _____
4. ☐ movie theater ☐ mall ☐ funny ☐ park _____
5. ☐ talk on the phone ☐ dangerous ☐ play video games ☐ watch DVDs _____
6. ☐ Internet ☐ messy ☐ boring ☐ interesting _____
7. ☐ Brazil ☐ Puerto Rico ☐ computer ☐ Canada _____

2 Complete the text with the verb phrases in the box.

☐ do my homework	☐ eat dinner	☑ get up	☐ go to school	☐ take dance lessons
☐ eat breakfast	☐ eat lunch	☐ go to bed	☐ listen to music	☐ watch TV

My name is Rose. Every day, I _get up_ at 5:30 A.M. At 6:30, I _____ with my family. Then I _____ . I walk with my sister and brother. I _____ with my friend, Katie, in the cafeteria. At 4:30, I _____ . I'm pretty good at dancing. At 6:30, I _____ in the dining room at home. Then I _____ . I don't like homework very much. I like music a lot. I _____ every night. Ilegales is my favorite band. I don't _____ . TV is boring. Then I _____ at 10:30.

3 Write sentences with your own information.

1. (play tennis) _I play tennis._ OR _I don't play tennis._
2. (watch TV) _____
3. (hang out at the park) _____
4. (in-line skate) _____
5. (write e-mail messages) _____
6. (get up at 6:00) _____
7. (talk on the phone) _____
8. (speak three languages) _____

1 Complete the chart with the correct forms of the verbs.

1. I work	she _works_	7. I live	she _____
2. I go	he _____	8. I take	he _____
3. I watch	she _____	9. I teach	she _____
4. I collect	he _____	10. I have	he _____
5. I guess	she _____	11. I make	she _____
6. I do	he _____	12. I practice	he _____

2 Complete the texts with the correct forms of the verbs in the box.

☐ do	☐ go	☐ listen	☐ talk	☐ work
☐ get up	☐ have	☑ live	☐ teach	☐ write

This is my cousin, Mary Ann. She's thirteen.
She ___lives___ in Texas. She _____ at
6:30 every day. Then she _____ to school.
Mary Ann _____ hard in school.
Mrs. Haywood is Mary Ann's favorite
teacher. Mrs. Haywood _____ music.

After school, Mary Ann _____ her
homework and _____ to music in her
room. She _____ a computer in her
room. At night, she _____ on the phone
or _____ e-mail messages to her friends.

3 Write sentences about your friends or family members.

1. (talk) _My brother talks on the phone every day._
2. (work) _____
3. (read) _____
4. (collect) _____
5. (have) _____
6. (go to bed) _____
7. (play) _____
8. (get up) _____

1 Write sentences about the things Jean doesn't do in her free time.

1. Jean plays video games.

   (the piano) *She doesn't play the piano.*

2. Jean eats out with her family.

   (her friends) _____

3. She goes to the movies with her sister.

   (her brother) _____

4. Jean likes candy.

   (popcorn) _____

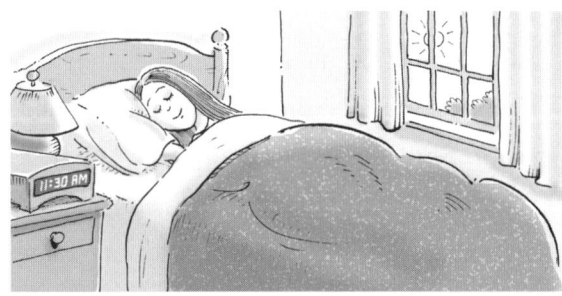

5. On Saturday, Jean sleeps late.

   (get up early) _____

6. She in-line skates in the park.

   (at school) _____

2 Write negative sentences with *doesn't*.

1. Adina watches TV in the dining room. *Adina doesn't watch TV in the dining room.*

2. He goes to the movies every Saturday. _____

3. Gregorio stays home on Sunday. _____

4. She sleeps late on Monday. _____

5. Julio talks on the phone at school. _____

6. Gina goes out on Friday night. _____

7. He hangs out at the mall. _____

8. She collects stamps. _____

Lesson 10 Connections

1 Complete the chart with the words in the box.

☐ dances ☐ eat lunch ☐ hang out ☐ practices
☑ draw ☐ gets up ☐ has ☐ work

I	he / she
draw	

2 Write sentences with the correct forms of the verbs.

1. I play the guitar.   (she) *She plays the guitar.* _____
2. I live in Tokyo.   (my sister) _____
3. Veronica goes to Oak Street School. (I) _____
4. Mrs. Amato teaches science.   (he) _____
5. I don't work at the mall.   (Taro) _____
6. Gabriel has a sister and a brother. (Maria) _____

3 Look at the pictures. Then write sentences about Guillermo and Linda.

1. (sleep late)
   Guillermo sleeps late. _____

2. (play tennis)
   _____

3. (play the violin)
   _____

4. (have a computer)
   _____

5. (collect stamps)
   _____

1. (sleep late)
   Linda doesn't sleep late. _____

2. (play tennis)
   _____

3. (play the violin)
   _____

4. (have a computer)
   _____

5. (collect stamps)
   _____

Lesson 11 Sports fun

1 Ann and Kay talk about their new gym teacher. Write conversations.

Ann *Does he play soccer?*   Ann _____   Ann _____
Kay *No, he doesn't.*   Kay _____   Kay _____

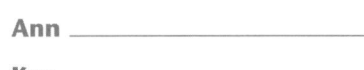

Ann _____   Ann _____   Ann _____
Kay _____   Kay _____   Kay _____

2 Write questions and answers.

1. **Q:** (Miss Alverez / do karate) *Does Miss Alverez do karate?*
   A: (yes) *Yes, she does.*

2. **Q:** (he / ski) _____
   A: (no) _____

3. **Q:** (Hiro / go biking) _____
   A: (yes / he) _____

4. **Q:** (Sarah / water-ski) _____
   A: (no / she) _____

5. **Q:** (she / surf) _____
   A: (yes) _____

6. **Q:** (Raul / skateboard) _____
   A: (no / he) _____

7. **Q:** (Angela / swim) _____
   A: (yes / she) _____

8. **Q:** (Mr. Miller / play baseball) _____
   A: (yes) _____

12 Sports equipment

1 Write questions and answers.

1. (skiers / gloves)

   Q: *Do skiers wear gloves?*

   A: *Yes, they do. Skiers wear gloves.*

2. (cyclists / ski boots)

   Q: _____

   A: _____

3. (skateboarders / knee pads)

   Q: _____

   A: _____

4. (basketball players / hats)

   Q: _____

   A: _____

5. (swimmers / goggles)

   Q: _____

   A: _____

6. (baseball players / uniforms)

   Q: _____

   A: _____

7. (soccer players / hats)

   Q: _____

   A: _____

8. (cyclists / helmets)

   Q: _____

   A: _____

2 Complete the conversation. Write questions with *Do they* and the verb phrases in the box.

☐ play on a field   ☐ wear goggles   ☑ wear uniforms
☐ use knee pads   ☐ wear helmets

Jim Let's play a game. Guess my favorite sports team!

Andy OK. Let's see. Tell me about the players.

   Do they wear uniforms?

Jim Yes, they do. They wear team uniforms.

Andy _____

Jim No, they don't wear helmets.

Andy _____

Jim No, they don't wear goggles.

Andy Wow! This is hard.

   _____

Jim No, they don't. They don't use knee pads.

Andy _____

Jim No, they don't. They play on a court.

Andy Aha! Are they basketball players?

Jim Yes, they are! Our school basketball team is my
favorite. I'm on the team!

Mini-review

1 Check (✓) the word or phrase that is different. Then write one more correct word or phrase.

1.	☐ basketball	☐ soccer	✓ piano	☐ tennis	_baseball_
2.	☐ knee pads	☐ stamps	☐ goggles	☐ gloves	_____
3.	☐ uniform	☐ eyes	☐ feet	☐ head	_____
4.	☐ athletic	☐ smart	☐ use	☐ artistic	_____
5.	☐ skateboarder	☐ baseball player	☐ swimmer	☐ hat	_____
6.	☐ swim	☐ write	☐ surf	☐ water-ski	_____
7.	☐ park	☐ field	☐ helmet	☐ court	_____
8.	☐ active	☐ go out	☐ sleep late	☐ stay home	_____

2 Number the sentences in the correct order.

_____ No, he doesn't water-ski. But he skis in the winter.

_____ Does he surf?

_1_ Hey, there's Antonio. He swims really well.

_____ Wow! He does a lot!

_____ Yeah, he's a good swimmer. He really likes the water.

_____ Yes, he's very athletic. He does a lot of sports.

_____ Every day? Wow! Does he water-ski, too?

_____ Yes, he does. He surfs every day in the summer.

3 Circle the correct words to complete the questions. Then write answers.

1. **A** (Do / Does) your friends play soccer?
   B (yes) _Yes, they do._

2. **A** (Do / Does) you have goggles?
   B (no) _____

3. **A** (Do / Does) your parents use the Internet?
   B (yes) _____

4. **A** (Do / Does) your English teacher wear a hat?
   B (no) _____

4 Complete the questions with *do* or *does*. Then answer the questions with your own information.

1. _Do_ you like English? _Yes, I do._

2. _____ your mother water-ski? _____

3. _____ your best friend surf? _____

4. _____ your classmates like homework? _____

Lesson 13 Off to camp

1 Unscramble the words.

1. n k i h i g t o b o s   *hiking boots*
2. p o s a   _____
3. l o w t e   _____
4. g u b n e p r e l e l t   _____
5. w i l p o l   _____
6. r e s s c u n n e   _____
7. i c t r o a n a   _____
8. e k l t n a b   _____
9. p e i l s n e g g b a   _____
10. t h a s h l l g i f   _____

2 What are the rules at camp? Write sentences.

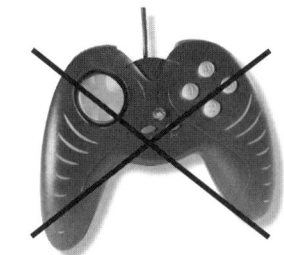

1. (play)

Don't play video games.

2. (use)

_____

3. (bring)

_____

4. (wear)

_____

5. (use)

_____

6. (bring)

_____

3 What are the rules in your class? Write imperatives.

1. (cell phones) *Don't bring cell phones.*

2. (radios)   _____

3. (video games)   _____

4. (the Internet)   _____

5. (homework)   _____

6. (comic books)   _____

7. (guitar)   _____

8. (magazines)   _____

Sports and Activities 17

Lesson 14 At camp

1 Look at Marco's camp schedule. Answer the questions.

9:30 – go canoeing	3:15 – do arts and crafts
10:45 – take swimming lessons	6:00 – make a campfire
12:30 – go horseback riding	6:30 – cook hot dogs
1:45 – go hiking	8:00 – tell stories

1. What time does Marco go canoeing? _He goes canoeing at 9:30._ OR _At 9:30._

2. When do the campers make a campfire? _____

3. What time does Marco go horseback riding? _____

4. What time do the campers go hiking? _____

5. When do they tell stories? _____

6. When does Marco take swimming lessons? _____

7. What time does Marco cook hot dogs? _____

8. When do they do arts and crafts? _____

2 Write the time of day.

1. 9 P.M. _in the evening_   3. 11 A.M. _____   5. 3 P.M. _____

2. 4 A.M. _____   4. 6 A.M. _____   6. 12 A.M. _____

3 Write questions and answers.

1. **Q:** (your parents / get up) _When do your parents get up?_
   A: (in the morning) _My parents get up in the morning._ OR _In the morning._

2. **Q:** (your friends / eat lunch) _____
   A: (in the afternoon) _____

3. **Q:** (your classmates / go home) _____
   A: (2:30) _____

4. **Q:** (your teacher / use his computer) _____
   A: (in the morning) _____

5. **Q:** (your sister / go to bed) _____
   A: (10:30) _____

6. **Q:** (your best friend / do homework) _____
   A: (in the evening) _____

Lesson 15 Connections

1 Unscramble the questions. Then answer the questions with your own information.

1. math teacher / Does / soccer / play / your ?

   Q: *Does your math teacher play soccer?*　　　　**A:** *No, he doesn't.*

2. Does / surf / your / best friend ?

   Q: _____　　　　**A:** _____

3. your / lunch / do / eat / What / classmates / time ?

   Q: _____　　　　**A:** _____

4. English teacher / When / get / does / up / your ?

   Q: _____　　　　**A:** _____

5. your / wear / Do / school / knee pads / players / at / soccer ?

   Q: _____　　　　**A:** _____

6. the / sunscreen / Do / use / at / your / beach / friends ?

   Q: _____　　　　**A:** _____

2 Write imperatives. 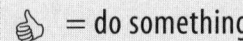 = do something　　 = don't do something

1. 👍 / wear

   Wear a helmet.

2. 👍 / use

   _____

3. 👎 / wear

   _____

4. 👎 / use

   _____

5. 👍 / bring

   _____

6. 👎 / use

   _____

16 I like music.

1 Unscramble the words. Then check (✓) the types of music that you like.

☐ 1. z a z j _____*jazz*_____
☐ 2. o p p _____
☐ 3. o y u c t n r _____
☐ 4. c o r k _____
☐ 5. g a r g e e _____
☐ 6. a a c c l l s s i _____

2 Match the questions to the answers.

1. Do you listen to jazz? __*d*__
2. Do you like classical music? ____
3. Do you like the Backstreet Boys? ____
4. What's your favorite kind of music? ____
5. Who's your favorite country singer? ____
6. Who's your favorite musician? ____

a. Martina McBride is my favorite country singer. I like her a lot.
b. My favorite musician is Yo-Yo Ma. I really like him.
c. Reggae is my favorite kind of music. I really like it!
d. Yes, I do. Jazz is cool. I like it.
e. No, I don't. Classical music is boring.
f. Yes, they're OK. I like them.

3 Choose the correct words to complete the sentences.

1. Shaggy is my favorite singer. I like __*him*__ (him / it) a lot.
2. The Beastie Boys are cool. I like _____ (them / him) a lot.
3. I don't like rock music at all. I don't listen to _____ (them / it).
4. Hip-hop singers are OK. I like _____ (her / them).
5. Pop music is great! I like _____ (her / it) a lot.
6. Jennifer Lopez is a good singer. I like _____ (them / her).

4 Answer the questions with your own information.

1. Do you like English? *Yes, I do. I like it a lot!*
2. Do you like the Red Hot Chili Peppers? _____
3. Do you like video games? _____
4. Do you like movies? _____
5. Do you like music videos? _____
6. Do you like Shaggy? _____
7. Do you like baseball? _____
8. Do you like pop music? _____

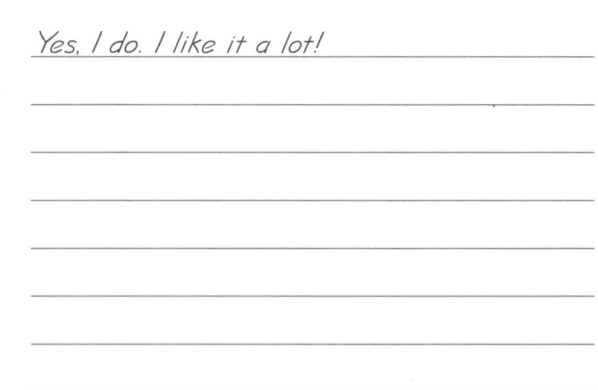

Unit 4 My Interests

Lesson 17 Let's look online.

1 Look at the picture. Then write questions.

1. **Q:** _How much are the puzzles?_
   A: They're $3.99 each.

2. **Q:** _____
   A: It's $89.75.

3. **Q:** _____
   A: They're $29.95 each.

4. **Q:** _____
   A: They're $18.00 each.

5. **Q:** _____
   A: It's $79.50

6. **Q:** _____
   A: They're $12.98 each.

7. **Q:** _____
   A: It's $99.99.

8. **Q:** _____
   A: It's $69.25.

2 Unscramble the questions. Then look at the picture and answer the questions.

1. CDs / much / are / How / the ?
   Q: _How much are the CDs?_
   A: _They're $13.99 each._

2. is / How / the / much / skateboard ?
   Q: _____
   A: _____

3. How / video games / are / the / much ?
   Q: _____
   A: _____

4. the / books / How / are / much ?
   Q: _____
   A: _____

2. much / the / guitar / How / is ?
   Q: _____
   A: _____

3. space map / is / the / much / How ?
   Q: _____
   A: _____

My Interests 21

1 Check (✓) the correct responses.

1. Do you like classical music?
   - ☑ Yes, I do. I like it a lot.
   - ☐ Yes, I do. I like them a lot.

2. Do you listen to the Dixie Chicks?
   - ☐ Yes, I do. I like her.
   - ☐ No, I don't. I don't like them.

3. Who's your favorite hip-hop singer?
   - ☐ LL Cool J. I really like it.
   - ☐ LL Cool J is great. I really like him.

4. Do you like Madonna?
   - ☐ No, I don't. She's weird.
   - ☐ They're boring. I don't like them at all.

5. What's your favorite kind of music?
   - ☐ Reggae is my favorite. I like him a lot.
   - ☐ Reggae is great. I really like it.

6. What's your favorite rock group?
   - ☐ The Goo-Goo Dolls are cool. I like them.
   - ☐ The Goo-Goo Dolls are weird. I don't like them at all.

7. Do you listen to Laura Pausini?
   - ☐ No, I don't. I don't like it.
   - ☐ No, I don't. I don't really like her.

8. Do you like Justin Timberlake?
   - ☐ Yes, I do. He's my favorite.
   - ☐ Not really. They're boring.

2 Complete the questions with *How much is* or *How much are.*

1. *How much is* the CD?
2. _____ the goggles?
3. _____ the radio?
4. _____ the calendar?
5. _____ the travel vests?
6. _____ the adventure DVD?

3 Look at the information. Are these statements true or false? Write *T* (true) or *F* (false). Then correct the false statements.

1. The flashlights are $13.95 each. *F*
   They're $8.69 each.

2. The hiking boots are $69.00. _____
   _____

3. The soccer ball is $18.66. _____
   _____

4. The space maps are $49.22 each. _____
   _____

5. The experiment kit is $24.99. _____
   _____

6. The music books are $19.35 each. _____
   _____

7. The radio-controlled airplane is $79.00. _____
   _____

- ☐ experiment kit $24.99
- ☑ flashlights $8.69 each
- ☐ hiking boots $69.00
- ☐ music books $13.95 each
- ☐ radio-controlled airplane $89.00
- ☐ soccer ball $16.88
- ☐ space maps $22.49 each

Lesson 18 Our interests

1 Write sentences. ✓ = like to / likes to ✖ = don't like to / doesn't like to

1. go camping ✓ / go shopping ✖

   I _like to go camping. I don't like_
   to go shopping.

2. ski ✓ / do crossword puzzles ✖

   I _____

   _____

3. write poetry ✓ / play tennis ✖

   He _____

   _____

4. play video games ✓ / practice the piano ✖

   She _____

   _____

5. go dancing ✓ / watch TV ✖

   She _____

   _____

6. go to the movies ✓ / do my homework ✖

   I _____

   _____

7. in-line skate ✓ / read magazines ✖

   I _____

   _____

8. spend time at the beach ✓ / hang out at the mall ✖

   He _____

   _____

2 Complete the sentences with *like to* or *don't like to* and the verb phrases in the box.

| do crossword puzzles | go camping | go shopping | listen to music |

Eddie Hey, Al. What's that?

Al Hi, Eddie. It's a crossword puzzle.

   I _like to do crossword puzzles._ They're interesting.

Eddie Me, too. I really like the outdoors, too.

   I _____ in my free time. How about you?

Al Not me. I don't like the outdoors, so I

   _____ . I like indoor activities.

Eddie Do you like to listen to music?

Al Yes, I do. I _____ . Rock and reggae are my favorites.

Eddie What don't you like to do?

Al That's easy. I _____ with my sister. She hangs out at the mall all day!

19 In and out of school

1 Unscramble the words. Then match the words to make verb phrases.

1. m e o c   *come* •
2. t e g   _____ •
3. o d   _____ •
4. w r o t h   _____ •
5. r e a n w s _____ •
6. p l e s e   _____ •

• paper airplanes
• my homework
• to class on time
• a lot of the teacher's questions
• in class
• good grades

2 Choose the correct words to complete the sentences.

1. *Sometimes* (Sometimes / Hardly ever) I like to hang out with my best friend.

2. I love country music. I _____ (never / always) listen to Shania Twain.

3. I'm not very athletic. I _____ (hardly ever / always) play sports.

4. I like to watch TV. I _____ (usually / never) watch TV every night.

5. Rock music is boring. I _____ (always / hardly ever) listen to it.

6. In my free time, I _____ (never / usually) spend time at the beach. I love the beach!

7. I like video games. I _____ (sometimes / hardly ever) play them.

8. I go to school at 7:30 in the morning. I _____ (always / never) sleep late on weekdays.

3 Write sentences. Use your own information and *always, usually, sometimes, hardly ever,* or *never.*

1. (throw paper airplanes in English class)

   I never throw paper airplanes in English class.

2. (sing in class) _____

3. (get good grades) _____

4. (skateboard) _____

5. (listen to music) _____

6. (spend time at the beach) _____

7. (come to class on time) _____

8. (do karate) _____

Lesson 20 Connections

1 Write sentences about Brad.   👍 = like to   👎 = don't like to

Hi. I'm Brad. I'm a very active person. I like to do a lot of things.

1. get up early 👍 / sleep late 👎   *I like to get up early. I don't like to sleep late.*

2. go camping 👍 / do crossword puzzles 👎 _____

3. stay home 👎 / go out with my friends 👍 _____

4. go dancing 👍 / go shopping 👎 _____

5. write poetry 👎 / spend time at the beach 👍 _____

6. watch TV 👎 / play sports 👍 _____

2 Look at the pictures. Then write sentences.

1. (I / hardly ever)
   I hardly ever write
   poetry.

2. (I / sometimes)
   _____
   _____

3. (we / never)
   _____
   _____

4. (they / usually)
   _____
   _____

5. (she / always)
   _____
   _____

6. (he / sometimes)
   _____
   _____

7. (we / hardly ever)
   _____
   _____

8. (he / always)
   _____
   _____

Lesson 21 In San Francisco

1 Label the pictures with the verb phrases in the box.

☐ go sightseeing   ☐ see a show   ☐ take pictures
☑ ride a trolley   ☐ take a boat ride ☐ walk in the park

1. _ride a trolley_

2. _____

3. _____

4. _____

5. _____

6. _____

2 Write these sentences in the present continuous.

1. You walk. _You're walking._   5. She goes. _____

2. They buy. _____   6. I write. _____

3. We take. _____   7. They do. _____

4. I ride. _____   8. We practice. _____

3 Write these sentences in the present continuous.

1. (I / take a boat ride) _I'm taking a boat ride._

2. (he / buy souvenirs) _____

3. (we / go sightseeing) _____

4. (she / walk in the park) _____

5. (they / see a show) _____

6. (I / take pictures) _____

7. (you / visit a museum) _____

8. (we / ride a trolley) _____

4 What are you doing right now? Write four sentences in the present continuous. Use your own information.

1. _____   3. _____

2. _____   4. _____

Lesson 22 At the park

1 Complete the sentences to make negative statements. Use the correct forms of the verb phrases in the box.

> ☑ eat in the picnic area ☐ stand in line ☐ throw trash in the trash can
> ☐ sit down in the boat ☐ stay on the bike path ☐ wait for the green light

1. They _aren't eating in the picnic area_ .

2. She _____ .

3. He _____ .

4. I'm _____ .

5. We _____ .

6. He _____ .

2 Write sentences.   ✓ = is doing something   ✖ = isn't doing something

1. he / pay attention ✖ / read a comic book ✓

   He isn't paying attention. He's reading a comic book.

2. we / follow the rules ✖ / throw paper airplanes ✓

   _____

3. I / read a magazine ✖ / use the Internet ✓

   _____

4. she / write poetry ✖ / listen to music ✓

   _____

5. they / stand in line ✖ / walk in the park ✓

   _____

6. he / practice the piano ✖ / play video games ✓

   _____

1 Complete the crossword puzzle with the words in the box.

☐ bike ☐ picnic ☐ show ☐ standing ☐ visiting
☐ boat ☐ pictures ☑ souvenirs ☐ trash ☐ waiting

Across
3. We're buying ____souvenirs____ .
5. They're seeing a _____ .
7. He isn't staying on the _____ path.
9. I'm _____ in line.
10. She's taking _____ .

Down
1. She isn't sitting down in the _____ .
2. I'm throwing _____ in the trash can.
4. They're _____ a museum.
6. We aren't _____ for the green light.
8. He's eating in the _____ area.

2 Look at the pictures. Then write sentences in the present continuous.

1. Pedro and José / in-line skate

   Pedro and José aren't in-line skating. They're skateboarding.

2. Mia / stand in line

   _____

3. Cesar / walk in the park

   _____

4. Denise and Julia / eat in the picnic area

   _____

5. Raul / talk on a cell phone

   _____

6. Sherri / throw paper airplanes

   _____

Lesson 23 At the beach

1 Answer the questions.

1. Is he playing in the sand?

   No, he isn't. He's swimming in the ocean.

2. Are they collecting seashells?

   _____

3. Are they flying a kite?

   _____

4. Is she floating on a raft?

   _____

5. Is he playing in the sand?

   _____

6. Are they surfing?

   _____

2 Write questions and answers.

1. **Q:** (Scott / play in the sand) _Is Scott playing in the sand?_   **A:** (no) _No, he isn't._

2. **Q:** (Linda / float on a raft) _____   **A:** (yes) _____

3. **Q:** (Josh and Brian / sail a boat) _____   **A:** (no) _____

4. **Q:** (Sally / collect seashells) _____   **A:** (yes) _____

5. **Q:** (Alberto / swim in the ocean) _____   **A:** (no) _____

6. **Q:** (Natalie and Sasha / have a picnic) _____   **A:** (yes) _____

Favorite Activities 29

24 At the store

1 Find and circle the words in the puzzle. Look in these directions (→, ↓, ↘).

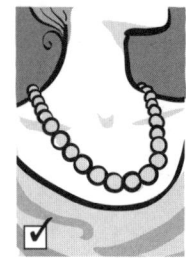  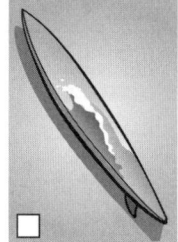   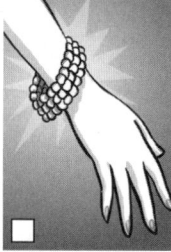

☑ ☐ ☐ ☐ ☐ ☐

S	B	R	A	C	E	L	E	T	N
N	U	Y	I	L	K	T	D	C	E
E	Z	R	I	N	G	M	O	P	C
C	F	I	F	S	N	H	K	V	K
D	O	N	C	B	J	E	S	B	L
C	Q	A	R	E	O	G	C	E	A
V	P	U	T	Z	W	A	A	L	C
G	N	Z	U	T	Q	V	R	W	E
Y	L	S	D	R	H	J	F	D	V

2 Read the answers. Look at the underlined words. Then write questions.

1. **Q:** _What are you doing?_

   A: I'm <u>shopping for</u> a hat.

2. **Q:** _____

   A: She's <u>buying</u> a bracelet.

3. **Q:** _____

   A: They're <u>looking at</u> surfboards.

4. **Q:** _____

   A: He's <u>trying on</u> a coat.

5. **Q:** _____

   A: She's <u>paying for</u> a necklace.

6. **Q:** _____

   A: I'm <u>buying</u> a tennis racket.

Connections

1 Complete the conversations with the correct forms of the verbs in the box.

☑ buy	☐ play	☐ see	☐ swim	☐ try	☐ walk
☑ do	☐ sail	☐ shop	☐ take	☐ visit	☐ watch

1. **A** What's your sister _doing_?
   B She's _buying_ souvenirs.

2. **A** Are Pete and Mike _____ in the ocean?
   B No, they aren't. They're _____ a boat.

3. **A** Is Marty _____ a museum?
   B No, he isn't. He's _____ in the park.

4. **A** Are you _____ TV?
   B No, we aren't. We're _____ video games.

5. **A** What's Elaine _____ on?
   B She's trying on a bracelet. She's _____ for jewelry.

6. **A** Is Christina _____ a boat ride?
   B No, she isn't. She's _____ a show.

2 Look at the picture. Then write sentences.

1. Mr. Velez / listen to music

   Mr. Velez isn't listening to music. He's reading.

2. Kim / have a picnic

   _____

3. Jorge and Alicia / float on a raft

   _____

4. Eric / stand in line

   _____

5. Pilar / eat in the picnic area

   _____

Unit 6 Entertainment

1 Look at the ads. Then write questions.

1. **Q:** _____

   A: She's going to a concert.

2. **Q:** _____

   A: They're going to an animal exhibit.

3. **Q:** _____

   A: He's going to the movies.

4. **Q:** _____

   A: I'm going to the circus.

OAK PARK HIGH

Science Exhibit

5. **Q:** _____

   A: We're going to a soccer game.

6. **Q:** _____

   A: She's going to a science exhibit.

2 Write questions and answers with *be + going to*.

1. (Amy / the museum)

   Q: *Where's Amy going?*

   A: *She's going to the museum.*

2. (Mr. Parker / a concert)

   Q: _____

   A: _____

3. (Ava and Jenna / the mall)

   Q: _____

   A: _____

4. (you and Roberto / the soccer game)

   Q: _____

   A: _____

Birthday parties!

1 **Write the sentences in the present continuous.**

1. We usually eat at home. (restaurant / now) _We're eating at a restaurant now._

2. He usually does homework. (write poetry / today) _____

3. They usually relax at home. (go to the movies / tonight) _____

4. I usually sing songs. (listen to music / now) _____

5. His sisters usually play cards. (go out with friends / today) _____

6. We usually watch TV. (play party games / tonight) _____

7. They usually play baseball. (do karate / now) _____

8. She usually eats pizza. (eat cake / tonight) _____

2 **It's Saturday at 11 A.M. Look at the chart. Then write sentences.**

Name	Usually	Now
1. Antonio	sleep late	play cards
2. Tomas	watch TV	swim
3. Jack	do his homework	read a book
4. Marla	talk on the phone	listen to music
5. Kelly	relax at home	hang out at the mall
6. Jane	read magazines	use the Internet

1. _Antonio usually sleeps late. He's playing cards now._

2. _____

3. _____

4. _____

5. _____

6. _____

3 **What do you do on your birthday? Write sentences with your own information.**

1. _____

2. _____

3. _____

4. _____

5. _____

6. _____

Entertainment 33

Lessons 26&27 Mini-review

1 Complete the sentences with the correct forms of the verbs.

1. Look! The athlete ___is talking___ (talk) to her fans now.
2. Ashley usually _____ (stay) home on Saturday.
3. My sisters sometimes _____ (watch) TV after school.
4. Tom _____ (celebrate) his birthday now.
5. Gina _____ (eat) dinner at a restaurant now.
6. We usually _____ (have) a barbecue on Sunday.

2 Look at the pictures. Then write questions and answers.

Lisa

Mrs. Lee

Mr. Hall

Greg and Jill

1. **Q**: _Where's Lisa going?_

   A: _She's going to the shoe store._

2. **Q**: _____

   A: _____

3. **Q**: _____

   A: _____

4. **Q**: _____

   A: _____

3 What do these people do on the weekend? Look at the information in the chart. Are these statements true or false? Write *T* (true) or *F* (false). Then correct the false statements.

Name	Usually	Now	Name	Usually	Now
1. Erica	watch TV	read a book	4. Edwin	eat dinner at home	eat at a restaurant
2. Alanna	play cards	sing songs	5. Kevin	practice the piano	float on a raft
3. Scott	skateboard	play video games	6. Alysha	go to the library	go to the circus

1. Erica usually reads books.   _F_   _Erica usually watches TV. She's reading_
   a book now.

2. Alanna is playing cards now. ___ _____

3. Scott is skateboarding now. ___ _____

4. Edwin usually eats at a restaurant. ___ _____

5. Kevin is floating on a raft now. ___ _____

6. Alysha usually goes to the circus. ___ _____

34 Unit 6

28 Let's see a movie.

1 Unscramble the sentences. Then number them in the correct order to make a conversation.

it / Is / interesting ?

_____   _____

thanks . / No, / see / comedy / a / I / want / to .

_____   _____

you / to / What / want / do / see ?

_____   _____

go / I / to / movies / the / want / to .
I want to go to the movies.   _1_

Amazing Elephants / to / a / I / documentary, / see / want .

_____   _____

it / Yes, / is . / come / Do / want / you / to ?

_____   _____

2 Look at the pictures. Then write sentences with *want to* and the words in the box.

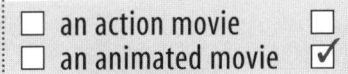  

☐ an action movie   ☐ a comedy   ☐ a drama
☐ an animated movie   ☑ a documentary   ☐ a horror movie

1. _We want to see a documentary._   2. **A** _____

                                          B Yes, I do.

3. _____   4. **A** _____

                                          B No, I don't.

5. _____   6. _____

Lesson 29 In line at the movies

1 Unscramble the words.

1. m i l s — *slim*
2. t h o r s _____
3. d o n l b _____
4. v e y h a _____
5. v y w a   i h a r _____

6. g l n o   r a h i _____
7. n r b o w   y e e s _____
8. l a t l _____
9. v a a g e e r   t h i g e h _____
10. g r t i h a t s   i a h r _____

2 Circle the correct words to complete the sentences. Then match the questions to the answers.

1. What (does)/ is) Tina look like? __b__
2. What's his (look / hair) like? ____
3. What (color / curly) is her hair? ____
4. What color (is / are) his eyes? ____
5. What does Ramon (is / look) like? ____

a. It's short and straight.
b. She's short and slim.
c. He's tall and heavy.
d. It's blond.
e. They're blue.

3 Write questions.

1. **Q:** (Aleta) _What does Aleta look like?_

   A: Aleta is average height and slim.

2. **Q:** (Don) _____

   A: They're blue.

3. **Q:** (Viviana) _____

   A: It's brown.

4. **Q:** (Allen) _____

   A: It's short and curly.

5. **Q:** (Paco) _____

   A: Paco is tall and heavy.

6. **Q:** (Sara) _____

   A: It's blond and wavy.

4 Answer the questions with your own information.

1. What do you look like? _____

2. What color are your eyes? _____

3. What's your hair like? _____

4. What color is your hair? _____

1 Check (✓) the word or phrase that is different. Then write one more correct word or phrase.

1. ☐ a comedy   ☑ a singer   ☐ a drama   ☐ a horror movie   *an action movie*
2. ☐ artistic   ☐ heavy   ☐ tall   ☐ average height   _____
3. ☐ black   ☐ blond   ☐ popular   ☐ red   _____
4. ☐ animal   ☐ amazing   ☐ fascinating   ☐ awesome   _____
5. ☐ circus   ☐ concert   ☐ exhibit   ☐ wavy   _____
6. ☐ eat cake   ☐ open presents   ☐ video games   ☐ sing songs   _____

2 Complete the conversation with the sentences in the box.

> ☐ And what color are her eyes?   ☐ It's brown.   ☐ What color is her hair?
> ☐ He's tall and has short, blond hair.   ☐ She's tall and slim.   ☑ What does she look like?

Maya Where's Erica? She's late for soccer practice!

Sue Erica? *What does she look like?* _____

Maya _____

Sue A lot of girls are tall and slim. _____

Maya Her hair? _____

Sue _____

Maya Her eyes? I don't know!

Sue I think I see her. She's talking to a boy.

Maya A boy? What does he look like?

Sue _____

Maya Oh, he's cute! That's why she's late for practice!

3 Write questions and answers.

1. **Q**: (you / buy a book) *Do you want to buy a book?* _____
   A: Yes, I do.
2. **Q**: (you / see a musical) _____
   A: Yes, I do.
3. **Q**: (you / visit a museum) _____
   A: No, I don't.
4. **Q**: Do you want to see a horror movie?
   A: (no) _____
5. **Q**: Do they want to go sightseeing?
   A: (yes) _____

Lesson 31 I'm hungry!

1 Label the photos. Then write *C* if the food item is countable and *U* if the food item is uncountable.

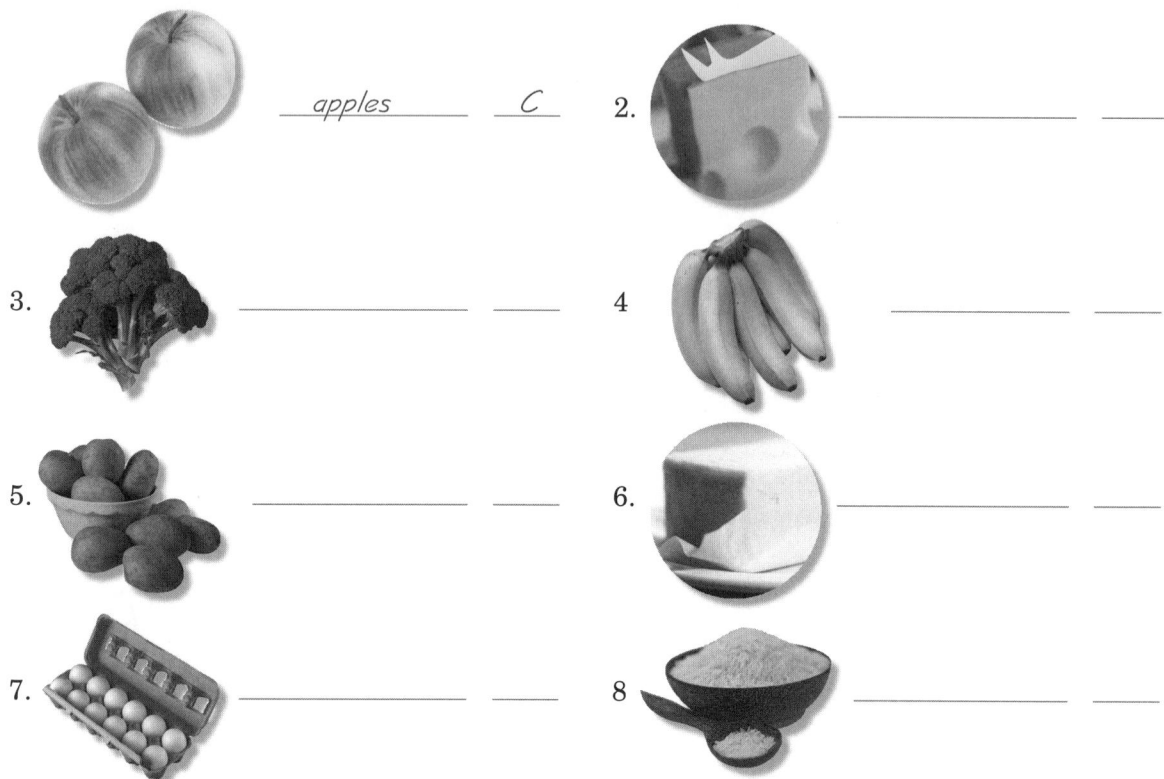

apples _C_ 2. _____ ____

3. _____ ____ 4 _____ ____

5. _____ ____ 6. _____ ____

7. _____ ____ 8 _____ ____

2 Choose the correct words to complete the sentences.

1. He's buying ____water____ (banana / water).
2. She wants _____ (meat / cookie) for dinner.
3. There are five _____ (broccoli / potatoes).
4. They don't eat _____ (hot dogs / egg).
5. There's _____ (butter / apples) on the table.
6. He's eating _____ (apple / rice).
7. How about a _____ (cheese / sandwich)?
8. I want five _____ (apples / meat).

3 Write sentences with the correct forms of the nouns and your own information.

1. (ice cream) _I like ice cream!_ _____
2. (banana) _____
3. (broccoli) _____
4. (butter) _____
5. (hot dog) _____
6. (cheese) _____

32 Picnic plans

1 Complete the sentences with *how much, how many, a little, a lot,* or *a few.*

1. _How many_ plates do we have?

5. There are _____ of knives and spoons.

2. There's _____ bread.

6. _____ cheese do we have?

3. We have _____ of pasta.

7. There are only _____ cups.

4. _____ milk is there?

8. _____ bananas do we need?

2 Look at the picture. Then write sentences about the quantities of the items with *We have.*

1. (fruit) _We have a lot of fruit._

4. (milk) _____

2. (forks) _____

5. (cups) _____

3. (pasta) _____

6. (spoons) _____

3 Write questions and answers. Use *Is there* or *Are there.*

1. (cups / five)

Q: _How many cups are there?_

A: _There are five cups._

2. (knives / eight)

Q: _____

A: _____

3. (forks / six)

Q: _____

A: _____

4. (juice / a little)

Q: _____

A: _____

5. (bread / a lot)

Q: _____

A: _____

6. (pasta / a lot)

Q: _____

A: _____

Mini-review

1 Look at the chart. Complete the questions. Then answer the questions.

Name	A lot	A little	A few
Alice	✔		
Jean and Joe			✔
Tony		✔	
Ivy and Jan	✔		
Nancy			✔
Ruben		✔	

1. **Q:** _How much bread_ does Alice have?
   A: _She has a lot of bread._

2. **Q:** _____ do Jean and Joe eat every day?
   A: _____

3. **Q:** _____ does Tony need?
   A: _____

4. **Q:** _____ do Ivy and Jan need?
   A: _____

5. **Q:** _____ does Nancy want?
   A: _____

6. **Q:** _____ does Ruben have at home?
   A: _____

2 Write questions with *How much* and *How many*.

1. **Q:** _How much juice do you drink every day?_

   A: I drink a little juice every day.

2. **Q:** _____

   A: I have three brothers.

3. **Q:** _____

   A: I eat a little fruit every morning.

4. **Q:** _____

   A: I read a few comic books every month.

5. **Q:** _____

   A: I eat two cookies after school.

6. **Q:** _____

   A: I drink a lot of water in the morning.

Lesson
33 A snack

1 **Number the sentences in the correct order.**

_____ Sorry, I don't like mayonnaise at all.

_____ Sure. Jelly burgers are my favorite!

_1_ Let's make hamburgers.

_____ I don't like mustard. Hey! There's some pepper and some jelly.

_____ That's okay. We have some mustard, but there isn't any ketchup.

_____ What? Jelly on a hamburger?

_____ Me, too. Let's use some mayonnaise.

_____ Good idea! I'm really hungry.

2 **Look at the picture. Then write sentences with *some* or *any*.**

1. _There aren't any sandwiches._

2. _____

3. _____

4. _____

5. _____

6. _____

3 **Are these items in your kitchen? Check (✓) Yes or No. Then write sentences.**

	Yes	No	
1. salt	✓	☐	_There's some salt._
2. jelly	☐	☐	
3. ketchup	☐	☐	
4. mayonnaise	☐	☐	
5. pepper	☐	☐	
6. ham	☐	☐	

Lesson 34 On the menu

1 Complete the chart with the words in the box.

☐ baked potato ☐ cheeseburger ☐ fish ☐ iced tea ☐ soda
☑ black bean soup ☐ chicken sandwich ☐ french fries ☐ milk shake ☐ steak sandwich
☐ carrot cake ☐ chocolate cake ☐ ice cream ☐ salad ☐ vegetable soup

Appetizers	Main dishes	Side orders	Desserts	Drinks
black bean soup	_____	_____	_____	_____
_____	_____	_____	_____	_____
_____	_____	_____	_____	_____
_____	_____	_____	_____	_____

2 Write questions and answers.

1. **Q:** (an appetizer) *Would you like an appetizer?*
   A: Yes, please. I'd like black bean soup.

2. **Q:** (drink) _____
   A: I'd like a milk shake.

3. **Q:** (ice cream) _____
   A: No, thanks. I don't like ice cream.

4. **Q:** Would you like a main dish?
   A: (fish) _____

5. **Q:** Would you like a side order?
   A: (no) _____

3 Unscramble the questions and answers. Then match each question to the correct answer.

1. a / like / you / Would / sandwich ?
   Would you like a sandwich?   *a*

2. you / like / Would / a / side order ?
   _____

3. vegetable soup / you / Would / some / like ?
   _____

4. some / Would / cake / like / chocolate / you ?
   _____

5. a / like / you / drink / Would ?
   _____

a. please . / Yes, / a / I'd / like / steak sandwich .
   Yes, please. I'd like a steak sandwich.

b. please . / Yes, / really / I'm / thirsty .

c. thanks . / No, / don't / cake . / chocolate / like / I

d. some / I'd / french fries / like .

e. please . / Yes, / vegetable soup / like / I'd / some .

1 Find the words in the box in the puzzle. Look in these directions (→, ↓).

☑ cake ☐ ham ☐ lettuce ☐ meat ☐ pie ☐ soda
☐ cookie ☐ jelly ☐ mayonnaise ☐ mustard ☐ salad ☐ soup

M	A	Y	O	N	N	A	I	S	E	G	H	A	M
U	R	W	Y	A	J	P	B	O	K	S	R	Z	P
S	A	L	A	D	Q	C	R	D	W	X	M	L	I
T	M	P	C	F	Y	A	L	A	Z	Q	N	Y	E
A	E	S	O	U	P	K	R	A	J	E	L	L	Y
R	A	B	X	Y	W	E	L	E	T	T	U	C	E
D	T	C	O	O	K	I	E	V	X	P	R	J	L

2 Look at the picture. Are the sentences true or false? Check (✓) T (true) or F (false). Then correct the false statements. Write sentences with *some* or *any*.

	T	F	
1. There's some water.	☐	☑	*There isn't any water.*
2. There aren't any bananas.	☐	☐	
3. There isn't any jelly.	☐	☐	
4. There isn't any bread.	☐	☐	
5. There isn't any ketchup.	☐	☐	
6. There's some ham.	☐	☐	

3 Complete the questions. Then answer them with your own information.

1. **Q:** *Would you like* some iced tea?   **A:** *Yes, please.*

2. **Q:** _____ a milk shake?   **A:** _____

3. **Q:** _____ some rice?   **A:** _____

4. **Q:** _____ some fish?   **A:** _____

5. **Q:** _____ french fries?   **A:** _____

36 World weather

1 **Unscramble the words. Then check (✓) the kinds of weather that you like.**

☐ 1. n u s y n _____sunny_____   ☐ 5. d w y n i _____

☐ 2. d o c l _____   ☐ 6. o l o c _____

☐ 3. o t h _____   ☐ 7. i r y n a _____

☐ 4. u c l y o d _____   ☐ 8. s w y n o _____

2 **Look at the pictures. Write sentences.**

1. _It's hot and sunny today._____   2. _____

3. _____   4. _____

5. _____   6. _____

3 **Write questions and answers.**

1. **Q:** (Chicago / January) _What's the weather like in Chicago in January?_

   A: It's usually cold and snowy.

2. **Q:** (Miami / August) _____

   A: It's usually hot and rainy.

3. **Q:** (New York City / today) _____

   A: It's cool and windy today.

4. **Q:** What's the weather like in Sydney in May?

   A: (cool / cloudy) _____

5. **Q:** What's the weather like in London in December?

   A: (cold / rainy) _____

6. **Q:** What's the weather like in Tokyo today?

   A: (warm / sunny) _____

Unit 8 The Natural World

Lesson 37 Natural wonders

1 Complete the sentences with the correct words.

1. You can climb an incredible ___mountain___ (river / mountain) in this park.
2. This _____ (island / cave) is usually hot and rainy in June.
3. Can you relax in a _____ (mountain / hot spring) in this park?
4. You can see bats in this _____ (hotel / cave).
5. You can live in a houseboat on a _____ (hot spring / river).

2 Write questions.

1. **Q:** _What can you see in a rain forest?_

   A: You can see fascinating birds and animals in a rain forest.

2. **Q:** _____

   A: Yes, you can. You can see bats in a cave.

3. **Q:** _____

   A: Yes, you can. You can buy food and souvenirs at hotels.

4. **Q:** _____

   A: No, you can't. You can't collect seashells in the mountains.

5. **Q:** _____

   A: You can see birds on this island.

6. **Q:** _____

   A: You can go camping in this park.

3 Answer the questions.

1. **Q:** Can you see bears on this trail?

   A: (no / snakes and spiders) _No, you can't. You can see snakes and spiders._

2. **Q:** Can you buy food around here?

   A: (yes / the hotel) _____

3. **Q:** What can you do on this river?

   A: (go canoeing) _____

4. **Q:** Can you go camping in this park?

   A: (no / hiking) _____

5. **Q:** What can you do in the hot spring?

   A: (sit and relax) _____

6. **Q:** What can you see on this island?

   A: (an underground cave) _____

1 Look at the chart. Then write questions and answers.

	Buenos Aires, Argentina	**Tokyo, Japan**
January	hot / rainy	cold / snowy
April	warm / cloudy	cool / cloudy
August	cool / sunny	hot / rainy
November	hot / cloudy	cool / cloudy

1. (Tokyo / April) *What's the weather like in Tokyo in April?*

    It's usually cool and cloudy.

2. (Buenos Aires / January) _____

    It's usually hot and rainy.

3. (Tokyo / August) _____

    It's usually hot and rainy.

4. What's the weather like in Buenos Aires in April?

    _____

5. What's the weather like in Tokyo in November?

    _____

2 Unscramble the questions. Then look at the pictures, and answer the questions.

1. park / you / see / can / What / this / in ?
    Q: *What can you see in this park?*
    A: *You can see hot springs in this park.*

2. see / birds / in / rain forest / Can / the / you ?
    Q: _____
    A: _____

3. cave / Can / in / go camping / you / a ?
    Q: _____
    A: _____

4. the / you / can / What / beach / at / do ?
    Q: _____
    A: _____

38 World of friends

1 **Match the questions to the answers.**

1. Who lives on a beautiful island? __d__

2. Who wants to learn German? _____

3. Who writes e-mail messages? _____

4. Who plays tennis? _____

5. Who watches French movies? _____

6. Who speaks Greek? _____

a. Kevin does. He writes to his e-pal every week!

b. Ashley and David do. They speak Italian, too.

c. I do! I watch American movies, too.

d. Yahaira does. She lives in Puerto Rico.

e. Frida does. She wants to visit Germany next year.

f. Sam and Mike do. They practice every day.

2 **Write answers with _do_ or _does_.**

1. Who uses the Internet?

   (Tammy) _Tammy does._

2. Who speaks German?

   (Tina and Jan) _____

3. Who lives in Portugal?

   (Rodrigo) _____

4. Who plays soccer?

   (I) _____

5. Who lives in Morocco?

   (you) _____

6. Who speaks English?

   (we) _____

3 **Look at the pictures. Then write questions and answers.**

Tony

Gina

Daniela and Laura

Frank

Dmitri

Jean

1. **Q:** _Who speaks Arabic?_

   A: Jean does.

2. **Q:** _____

   A: Frank does.

3. **Q:** _____

   A: Gina does.

4. **Q:** Who plays cards?

   A: _____

5. **Q:** Who skateboards?

   A: _____

6. **Q:** Who lives in Italy?

   A: _____

39 International Day

1 Write the numbers.

1. 589 *five hundred and eighty-nine*
2. 3,406 _____
3. 82,742 _____
4. 955,698 _____
5. 199 _____

6. 75,000 _____
7. 208,638 _____
8. 777 _____
9. 6,020 _____
10. 5,416 _____

2 Write questions and answers.

1. **Q:** (sports / you / like) *What sports do you like?* _____

   A: (baseball / basketball) *I like baseball and basketball.* _____

2. **Q:** (languages / your father / speak) _____

   A: (English / German) _____

3. **Q:** (instruments / they / play) _____

   A: (piano / guitar) _____

4. **Q:** (animals / your mother / like) _____

   A: (cats / dogs) _____

5. **Q:** (desserts / you / eat) _____

   A: (ice cream / cake / cookies) _____

6. **Q:** (subjects / you / like) _____

   A: (English / science / math) _____

3 Answer the questions with your own ir

1. What animals do you like?
   I like dogs and horses. _____

2. What languages do you speak?

   _____

3. What subjects do you like?

   _____

4. What foods do you eat?

   _____

5. What sports do you play?

   _____

6. What movies do you watch?

   _____

Lesson 40 Connections

1 Check (✓) the word or phrase that is different. Then write one more correct word or phrase.

1. ☐ Russian   ☐ Greek   ☑ fantastic   ☐ Arabic   *French*
2. ☐ funny   ☐ cloudy   ☐ rainy   ☐ windy   _____
3. ☐ cold   ☐ red   ☐ hot   ☐ warm   _____
4. ☐ Puerto Rico   ☐ hot spring   ☐ rain forest   ☐ cave   _____
5. ☐ January   ☐ November   ☐ July   ☐ weather   _____
6. ☐ go canoeing   ☐ go hiking   ☐ hotel   ☐ go camping   _____

2 Complete the conversations.

1. **A** (kinds of music / you / like) *What kinds of music do you like?*

   B I like pop and reggae.

2. **A** (animals / he / like) _____

   B He likes snakes and spiders.

3. **A** (sports / you / play) _____

   B I play tennis and soccer.

4. **A** (movies / they / watch) _____

   B They watch dramas and comedies.

5. **A** (kinds of weather / she / like) _____

   B She likes cold and snowy weather.

3 Look at the information. Write questions and answers about Alejandro and Mie.

Alejandro Perez
Santiago, Chile

• Speaks Spanish, English, and French
• Plays soccer and goes horseback riding

Mie Watanabe
Los Angeles, California

• Speaks English and Japanese
• Plays the violin and goes shopping with her friends

1. **Q:** *Who goes shopping with her friends?*   4. **Q:** _____

   A: *Mie does.*   **A:** _____

2. **Q:** _____   5. **Q:** _____

   A: _____   **A:** _____

3. **Q:** _____   6. **Q:** _____

   A: _____   **A:** _____

Check Yourself - Unit 1

A Complete the conversations with the sentences in the box.

☐ Are you in Mrs. Cook's class? ☐ She's twelve. ☑ Where are you from?
☐ It's in October. ☐ What's your name? ☐ Who are they?

1. **A** _Where are you from?_

   B I'm from Los Angeles.

2. **A** _____

   B My name's Regina.

3. **A** How old is she?

   B _____

4. **A** _____

   B They're my classmates.

5. **A** When's your birthday?

   B _____

6. **A** _____

   B No, I'm not.

B Complete the questions with *Is there a* or *Are there any*. Then look at the pictures, and answer the questions.

1. **Q:** _Is there a_
   swimming pool?

   A: _Yes, there is._

2. **Q:** _____
   restaurants?

   A: _____

3. **Q:** _____
   mall?

   A: _____

4. **Q:** _____
   tennis courts?

   A: _____

5. **Q:** _____
   gym?

   A: _____

6. **Q:** _____
   movie theater?

   A: _____

C Write sentences with *like* or *don't like*.

1. (I / dogs / a little) _I like dogs a little._

2. (I / rabbits / a lot) _____

3. (I / cats / at all) _____

4. (I / spiders / very much) _____

5. (I / snakes / at all) _____

6. (I / parrots / a lot) _____

Check Yourself-Unit 2

A Write sentences.

1. (Tess / in-line skate / after school) _Tess in-line skates after school._

2. (they / watch TV / 8:00) _____

3. (Kevin / take dance lessons) _____

4. (Bridget / go out / Friday night) _____

5. (my father / not teach music) _____

B Write questions. Then answer the questions with your own information.

1. **Q:** (collect stamps) _Do you collect stamps?_ _____

   A: _Yes, I do._ OR _No I don't._

2. **Q:** (listen to music) _____

   A: _____

3. **Q:** (play video games) _____

   A: _____

4. **Q:** (watch DVDs) _____

   A: _____

C Max talks about his day. What does he say? Look at the time line.
Check (✓) T (true) or F (false). Then correct the false sentences.

▲	▲	▲	▲	▲	▲	▲	▲
6:00	7:00	8:00	3:30	4:00	6:30	7:30	10:00
get up	eat breakfast at home	go to school with my sister	go home	play tennis	eat dinner	do homework	go to bed

	T	F	
1. I go to school with my mother.	☐	✓	_I don't go to school with my mother._ _I go to school with my sister._
2. I do my homework at 10:00.	☐	☐	_____
3. I eat breakfast at school.	☐	☐	_____
4. I play the piano at 4:00.	☐	☐	_____
5. I get up at 6:00.	☐	☐	_____

Check Yourself - Unit 3

A Circle the correct words to complete the sentences.

1. ((Don't listen to)/ Don't get up) your radio at night.
2. (Listen to / Wear) sunscreen.
3. (Get up / Bring) early.
4. (Don't use / Don't play) your cell phone.
5. (Wear / Play) something comfortable.
6. (Don't eat / Don't wear) french fries every day.
7. (Use / Play) bug repellent.
8. (Don't bring / Don't wear) a computer.

B Complete the sentences with *do*, *does*, *don't*, or *doesn't*.

1. **Q:** ___Do___ cyclists wear helmets?
   A: Yes, they ___do___ .

2. **Q:** _____ she play baseball?
   A: No, she _____ .

3. **Q:** _____ he do karate?
   A: Yes, he _____ .

4. **Q:** _____ they wear knee pads?
   A: No, they _____ .

5. **Q:** _____ you skateboard?
   A: Yes, I _____ .

6. **Q:** _____ he use the Internet at school?
   A: No, he _____ .

C Write questions and answers.

1. **Q:** (What time / he / go canoeing?) *What time does he go canoeing?* _____
   A: (8:15) *He goes canoeing at 8:15.* OR *At 8:15.* _____

2. **Q:** (When / she / do arts and crafts?) _____
   A: (in the afternoon) _____

3. **Q:** (What time / they / go hiking?) _____
   A: (10:00) _____

4. **Q:** (When / they / make a campfire?) _____
   A: (in the evening) _____

5. **Q:** (What time / she / go horseback riding?) _____
   A: (3:15) _____

6. **Q:** (When / he / tell stories?) _____
   A: (at night) _____

7. **Q:** (What time / you / take swimming lessons?) _____
   A: (9:30) _____

Check Yourself-Unit 4

A Rewrite the sentences with *her*, *him*, *it*, or *them*.

1. Mario likes Pink. _Mario likes her._

2. We like the Dixie Chicks a lot. _____

3. Peter doesn't like hip-hop. _____

4. I don't really like jazz. _____

5. Eric listens to Shaggy all the time. _____

6. She doesn't like Joshua Redman at all. _____

B Complete the questions with *How much is* or *How much are*. Then answer the questions.

1. **Q:** _How much is_____ the space map?

   A: ($12.75) _It's $12.75._____

2. **Q:** _____ the adventure DVDs?

   A: ($22.99 each) _____

3. **Q:** _____ the wall calendar?

   A: ($14.75) _____

4. **Q:** _____ the puzzles?

   A: ($8.00 each) _____

5. **Q:** _____ the travel vest?

   A: ($67.50) _____

6. **Q:** _____ the video sets?

   A: ($36.00 each) _____

C Complete the sentences with the correct words.

1. I _don't like to go_ (like to go / don't like to go) shopping. It's boring.

2. I'm a very active person. I _____ (like to spend / don't like to spend) time outdoors.

3. I don't like sports. I _____ (like to play / don't like to play) soccer.

4. I _____ (never / usually) go out on Saturdays. I hardly ever stay home.

5. I really like English class. I _____ (always / never) sleep in class.

6. I _____ (sometimes / hardly ever) eat hamburgers. I don't like them very much.

7. I like quiet, indoor activities. I _____ (like to write / don't like to write) poetry.

Check Yourself - Unit 5

A Write affirmative present continuous sentences.

1. (I / take pictures) _I'm taking pictures._
2. (they / visit a museum) _____
3. (she / ride a trolley) _____
4. (he / throw trash in the trash can) _____
5. (we / wait for the green light) _____
6. (you / buy souvenirs) _____

B Write negative present continuous sentences.

1. I'm staying on the bike path.

   (we) _We aren't staying on the bike path._

2. He's standing in line.

   (they) _____

3. They're playing in the sand.

   (she) _____

4. We're going sightseeing.

   (he) _____

5. She's eating in the picnic area.

   (I) _____

6. I'm visiting a museum.

   (you) _____

C Write questions with *Is* or *Are*. Then answer the questions.

1. **Q:** (she / look at jackets) _Is she looking at jackets?_

   A: (no / shoes) _No, she isn't. She's looking at shoes._

2. **Q:** (he / buy comic books) _____

   A: (no / a scarf) _____

3. **Q:** (they / collect seashells) _____

   A: (yes) _____

4. **Q:** (they / throw a Frisbee® disc) _____

   A: (no / fly a kite) _____

5. **Q:** (you / go sightseeing) _____

   A: (yes) _____

Check Yourself-Unit 6

A Write questions and answers.

1. **Q:** *Where are you going?*

   A: I'm going to the science exhibit.

2. **Q:** _____

   A: He's short and heavy.

3. **Q:** _____

   A: It's black.

4. **Q:** I want to go shopping. Do you want to come?

   A: (yes) _____

5. **Q:** Where's she going?

   A: (movie festival) _____

6. **Q:** What movie do you want to see?

   A: (action movie) _____

B Write sentences.

1. usually eat hamburgers / eat pizza now

   (we) *We usually eat hamburgers. We're eating pizza now.*

   _____

2. usually watch TV at night / go to a concert tonight

   (we) _____

3. usually read in the morning / hike today

   (Mr. Goldman) _____

   _____

4. usually sleep late / get up early today

   (Karla) _____

   _____

5. usually play baseball on Saturday / relax at home now

   (he) _____

   _____

6. usually hang out at the mall on Sunday / visit a museum now

   (they) _____

   _____

Check Yourself–Unit 7

A Complete these questions with *How much* or *How many*. Then match the questions to the answers.

1. _How many_ CDs do you have? _e_
2. _____ milk do we have? ____
3. _____ hours do you sleep every night? ____
4. _____ cups do we need? ____
5. _____ languages do you speak? ____
6. _____ soda do you drink every day? ____

a. I drink a lot of soda every day.
b. We need eight cups.
c. I speak three languages.
d. We have a little milk.
e. I have a lot of CDs.
f. I sleep eight hours every night.

B Complete the sentences with the correct words.

1. _There isn't_ (There isn't / There aren't) ____any____ (some / any) milk.

2. _____ (There's / There are) _____ (some / any) cups.

3. _____ (There are some / There's some) _____ (potatoes / potato).

4. _____ (There's some / There are some) _____ (eggs / egg).

5. _____ (There's / There are) _____ (some / any) ham.

C Write questions with *Would you like*. Then answer the questions with your own information.

1. **Q:** (dessert) _Would you like some dessert?_

   A: _Yes, please. I'd like some ice cream._

2. **Q:** (a drink) _____

   A: _____

3. **Q:** (a hamburger) _____

   A: _____

4. **Q:** (soup) _____

   A: _____

5. **Q:** (an appetizer) _____

   A: _____

6. **Q:** (pizza) _____

   A: _____

Check Yourself - Unit 8

A Complete the conversations with the questions in the box.

> ☐ Can you buy food at this hotel? ☐ What's the weather like in December?
> ☑ What can you see in this park? ☐ What's the weather like today?
> ☐ What movies do you like? ☐ Who hangs out at the mall after school?

1. **A** *What can you see in this park?*
   B You can see some incredible hot springs in this park.

2. **A** _____
   B It's warm and sunny today.

3. **A** _____
   B It's usually cold and snowy.

4. **A** _____
   B Marisol and Patricia do.

5. **A** _____
   B I like comedies and action movies.

6. **A** _____
   B Yes, you can.

B Look at the chart. Then write questions and answers about Ilsa and Eliot.

	Ilsa	**Eliot**
Sports	soccer, tennis	soccer, tennis
Movies	documentaries, dramas	action movies, comedies
Languages	English, German	English, German
Pets	dog, spiders	parrot

1. **Q:** (Eliot / watch) *What movies does Eliot watch?*
   A: *He watches action movies and comedies.*

2. **Q:** (Ilsa and Eliot / play) _____
   A: _____

3. **Q:** (Ilsa and Eliot / speak) _____
   A: _____

4. **Q:** (Ilsa / have) _____
   A: _____

Illustration Credits

Michael Brennan 9, 25, 34, 50
Andrea Champlin 26, 30, 43, 53
Laurie Conley 2, 13, 14, 23, 28, 39, 46, 47
Bruce Day 5, 11, 17, 27, 36, 38, 42, 52, 55, 56
Andrew Schiff 4, 6, 12, 19, 21, 31, 35, 41

Photographic Credits

3 *(both)* ©Corbis
4 ©Corbis
6 ©Tony Evans/Getty Images
7 *(clockwise from top left)* ©Corbis; ©Michael Krasowitz/Getty Images; ©Corbis; ©Picture Quest
10 *(top to bottom)* ©Getty Images; ©Corbis
11 ©Getty Images
13 ©Corbis
14 ©Corbis
15 ©Corbis
20 *(both)* ©Corbis
22 ©Index Stock
24 ©Jim Whitmer/Getty Images
25 ©Corbis
26 *(bottom)* ©Workbook Stock
30 ©Getty Images
32 *(clockwise from top left)* ©Thinkstock/Getty Images©Art Wolfe/Getty Images; ©Gary Randall/Getty Images; ©Alan Thornton/Getty Images; ©Photo Edit; ©Mike Powell/Getty Images; ©Deborah Davis/ Getty Images
33 ©Image State
37 *(top to bottom)* ©Corbis; ©Age Photo Stock
45 ©Stuart Westmorland/Getty Images
49 *(clockwise from top right)* ©Picture Quest; ©Corbis; ©Peter Cade/Getty Images
51 ©Lori Adamski Peek/Getty Images
53 ©Getty Images
54 ©Corbis
55 ©Getty Images

Notes

Notes

Notes

Notes